LIFE-CHANGING PRAYER

LIFE-CHANGING PRAYER

Approaching the Throne of Grace

STUDY GUIDE
SIX SESSIONS

JIM CYMBALA
WITH KEVIN AND SHERRY HARNEY

ZONDERVAN

Life-Changing Prayer Study Guide

This title is also available as a Zondervan ebook.

Requests for information should be addressed to:
Zondervan, *3900 Sparks Dr. SE, Grand Rapids, Michigan 49546*

ISBN 978-0-310-69484-7

Published in association with the literary agency of Ann Spangler and Company, 1415 Laurel Ave. SE, Grand Rapids, Michigan 49506.

Interior design: Kait Lamphere

First Printing December 2017 / Printed in the United States of America

Contents

A Word of Invitation

Have you ever been to Washington, D.C.? If so, you most likely drove or walked past the White House. And when you did, you probably noticed the fences, gates, security guards, and blockades. If you decided you wanted to chat with the president, you might find this difficult to do.

What do you think would happen if you tried to enter the White House uninvited? What if you climbed the fence? What if you decided you were going to ignore the warning signs, circumvent the guards, and just walk right into the Oval Office? At the absolute least, you would be deterred. You might even be tackled, restrained, and locked up for questioning.

We can be fairly confident that the same thing would happen if you decided to "visit" the queen of England during teatime and crash through the gates at Buckingham Palace. You would not get very far. This kind of thing is not allowed.

The president and the queen are just people, but they are very important people. Though they represent a nation, the citizens of that nation are not allowed to just pop by and knock on the door of their home. There are complex protocols and a whole list of rules and regulations that govern how you set up a meeting with such leaders.

If we are being sensible and honest, we would agree that it makes sense to have rules, regulations, and guidelines established when it comes to who can visit national dignitaries and leaders. An open-door policy is simply impractical for a president or queen.

What is truly amazing is that the King of Kings and Lord of the universe has an open-door policy with his children. If we have received the grace of God through faith in Jesus Christ, the door is open, his arms are spread wide, and the Maker of heaven and earth is always delighted for us to pop in and visit. As a matter of fact, those who have not yet received Jesus as their Savior also have an invitation to come in and talk with God any time.

Read these passages slowly and let their message sink deep into your soul:

> Let us then approach God's throne of grace with confidence, so that we may receive mercy and find grace to help us in our time of need. (HEBREWS 4:16)

> In him [Jesus] and through faith in him we may approach God with freedom and confidence. (EPHESIANS 3:12)

> Therefore, brothers and sisters, since we have confidence to enter the Most Holy Place by the blood of Jesus, by a new and living way opened for us through the curtain, that is, his body, and since we have a great priest over the house of God, let us draw near to God with a sincere heart and with the full assurance that faith brings, having our hearts sprinkled to cleanse us from a guilty conscience and having our bodies washed with pure water. (HEBREWS 10:19-22)

Are you getting the message? Is the picture becoming clear? The one God—Father, Son, and Holy Spirit—has invited you to draw near his throne of grace. No gates, no walls, no guards, no hours of operation, no "Keep Out" signs, no security cameras.

Jesus has made a way.
The throne room is waiting.
God's heart and arms are open.
Your name is on the guest list.
All you need to do is come.

How to Use This Guide

The *Life-Changing Prayer* video study is designed to be experienced in a group setting such as a Bible study, Sunday school class, or any small group gathering. Each session begins with a brief opening reflection and "talk about it" questions to get you and your group thinking about the topic. You will then watch a video with pastor Jim Cymbala and jump into some directed small-group discussion. You will close each session with a time of prayer as a group.

To get the most out of your group experience, keep the following points in mind. First, the real growth in this study will happen during your small-group time. This is where you will process the content of Jim Cymbala's message, ask questions, and learn from others as you hear what God is doing in their lives. For this reason, it is important for you to be fully committed to the group and attend each session so you can build trust and rapport with the other members. If you choose to only "go through the motions," or if you refrain from participating, there is a lesser chance you will find what you're looking for during this study.

Second, remember that the goal of your small group is to serve as a place where people can share, learn about God, and build intimacy and friendship. For this reason, seek to make your group a "safe place." This means being honest about your thoughts and feelings and listening carefully to everyone else's opinion. (If you are a group leader, there are additional instructions and resources in the back of the book for leading a productive discussion group.)

Third, resist the temptation to "fix" a problem someone might be having or to correct his or her theology, as that's not the purpose of your small-group time. Also, keep everything your group shares confidential. This will foster a rewarding sense of community in your group and create a place where people can heal, be challenged, and grow spiritually.

Following your group time, maximize the impact of the course with the additional between-session studies. For each session, you may wish to complete the personal study all in one sitting or spread it out over a few days (for example, working on it a half hour a day on four different days that week). Note that if you are unable to finish (or even start!) your between-sessions personal study, you should still attend the group study video session. You are still wanted and welcome at the group even if you don't have your "homework" done.

Keep in mind that the videos, discussions, and activities are simply meant to kick-start your imagination so you are not only open to what God wants you to hear but also how to apply it to your life. As you go through this study, be watching for what God is saying as it relates to approaching the throne of God's grace, receiving mercy, finding his peace, praying with faith, persevering in prayer for the answer, and praying together as a church.

OF NOTE

The quotations in this guide were taken from the video series and Jim Cymbala's teaching on prayer. The other resources in this guide—including the session introductions, small-group questions, and between-sessions materials—were written by Kevin and Sherry Harney in collaboration with Jim Cymbala. If you are a group leader, additional instructions and resources have been provided in the back of this guide to help you lead your group members through the study.

SESSION ONE

The Throne of Grace

The throne of grace is a spiritual place. It's not a location geographically that you can visit, but the promises concerning it are so immense that they're almost beyond belief. God has so much to say about the throne of grace and what will happen in our lives to change them for the better when we approach it in faith. All kinds of wonderful things happen at the throne of grace.

JIM CYMBALA

OPENING REFLECTION

If you could snap your fingers and be anywhere in the world immediately, where would you go? Some people would want to be transported to a childhood home. Others would want to be on a mountaintop or distant seashore. There are people who absolutely love the Disneyland theme parks, and they would want to go there. Some would want to stay near home and others would want to be on the other side of the planet.

Now, let's add to the fun of our imaginary instantaneous trip. Who would you want to take with you? It might be a spouse, a child, a grandchild, a friend, or maybe a group of people. Some folks might want to take someone they rarely get to see. Others might want to be reunited with a loved one who has passed away. Some creative people might decide to go to their imaginary place with a historical person they have never met. Since this is all imaginary, the sky is the limit. Any place. Any person.

Get the picture in your mind. With the snap of your fingers, you would be in the most desirable place with a favorite or fascinating person. How amazing would this be? What would you pay for this? How much joy would you experience? What stories would you have to tell when you were done and came back home?

The truth is, there is a place you can go that is better than your wildest imagination. There is someone already waiting there for you who is closer than your best friend, more loving than your kindest relative, more interesting than anyone you have met on this planet, and more generous than you can imagine or dream. There is a place you can go immediately, any time, and it costs you nothing to get there. And this place is not imaginary; in fact, it is the most real place in the entire universe.

The reason it costs nothing for you to go there is because someone else has already paid the fare. Jesus gave the full price so that you can have complete access to the God of the universe. This place is called *the throne of grace.* It is more beautiful than your wildest imagination can comprehend, and you will find a loving welcome every time you arrive.

Get ready. The way is open. It is stunning. God is waiting to welcome you. Are you ready to go?

TALK ABOUT IT

Welcome to the first session of Life-Changing Prayer. *If you or any of your fellow group members do not know one another, take a few minutes to introduce yourselves. Then, to get things started, discuss the following questions:*

- If you could go to any place on the planet right now, and have anyone there with you, where would you go? Whom would you meet there?
- Why would this be such a special time?

VIDEO TEACHING NOTES

Play the video segment for session one. As you watch, use the following outline to record any thoughts or concepts that stand out to you.

What happens at the throne of grace

Who may call on God at his throne of grace

The way to the throne of grace

The surprising provision and miracles we receive

Why we can ask God with confidence

We can know God is ready to meet us . . . now

My favorite Scripture is Jeremiah 29:11. God says in his Word, "'For I know the plans I have for you,' declares the LORD, 'plans to prosper you and not to harm you, plans to give you hope and a future.'" That Scripture helped me, because when I didn't have a plan for my life, I didn't have any hope. When everything around me seemed like it was harming me, God reminded me that he had a great plan for my life. It is not to harm me, but it is to prosper me. God is just so faithful. He has just been so faithful in my life. —SHERENE

GROUP DISCUSSION

Take a few minutes with your group members to discuss what you just watched and explore these concepts in Scripture.

1. Think about a time you felt God's presence in your life as you cried out to him. How did this experience affect you?

2. Read **Hebrews 4:14–16**. What do you learn about Jesus in this passage? How should these truths compel you to draw near the throne of grace frequently and confidently?

3. As you read this passage, what do you learn about how God sees you? Why is it essential for you to see yourself though God's eyes if you are going to draw near the throne of grace with absolute assurance that you are always welcome?

4. Read **Hebrews 10:19–25**. According to this passage, what has Jesus done to open the way for us to draw near the Father with confidence? Why is it essential that we remember the work and love of Jesus as we draw near the throne of grace?

5. Read **Hebrews 9:6–14**. What contrasts do you see between the human priests in the Old Testament and Jesus, the great and final High Priest? How is the ministry, sacrifice, and work of Jesus better than all that came before him?

6. Think about a time you drew near God, asked for his provision, and he showed up and provided in ways that only he could. Why is it important for you to remember and tell these stories of God's amazing provision and power?

7. God is not only concerned that you come to his throne of grace, but he also wants you to come with the right attitude and heart condition. What are some of the things that get in the way of you approaching God with a confident heart?

8. What prayer do you need to bring before God's throne of grace today? How can your group members approach God confidently with you and cry out with you to the loving God who is waiting for you to draw near?

CLOSING PRAYER

Use the following prompts to guide your group as you approach God's throne of grace together:

- Thank your heavenly Father that he has opened the door wide and invited you into his presence at all times.
- Give praise to Jesus for making the way for you to draw near through the willing sacrifice of his own life and through the power of his death-defeating resurrection.
- Pray for confidence and boldness to draw near the throne of grace as a normal part of your life.
- Cry out to God for a specific area of need, provision, or protection that has been shared by one of your group members.
- Lift up words of praise and adoration to the God who has made a way for you to be in intimate communication and relationship with him.

God is a rewarder of those who diligently seek him, who talk to him, and who ask him to help them.

Between-Sessions Personal Study

SESSION ONE

Reflect on the content you've covered this week in *Life-Changing Prayer* by engaging in any or all of the following between-sessions activities. The time you invest will be well spent, so let God use it to draw you closer to him. At your next meeting, share with your group any key points or insights that stood out to you as you spent this time with the Lord.

PERSONAL REFLECTION

Take time in personal reflection to think about the following questions:

- Think about when you first started calling out to God and seeking him in prayer. You might have been a child or an adult; a Christian or someone who was seeking the truth. What were your first prayers like? What happened in response to those prayers?

- What is keeping you from approaching God's throne of grace on a daily or even an hourly basis? What can you do to remove these roadblocks?

- How can you increase your confidence that God's door is always open and his arms are always ready to embrace you when you draw near?

- What might your day look like if you took time (even a few moments) to enter the throne room of God on a regular basis?

Outside of heaven, the most wonderful place to visit in the entire universe is called the throne of grace.

HIDE IT IN YOUR HEART

Take some time this week to commit this simple but powerful Bible verse to memory:

> Let us then approach God's throne of grace with confidence, so that we may receive mercy and find grace to help us in our time of need. (HEBREWS 4:16)

Then make this a prayer and personalize it:

> *My God, I approach your throne of grace with confidence, for I know there I will find mercy and grace to help me in any and every time of need!*

Pray this often, and then draw near to the God who is waiting for you and who is always excited when you come near.

Those who call upon the name of the Lord are answered by a God who has an ear that is never shut to their prayers.

GET TO KNOW THE HIGH PRIEST

One reason we may not draw near God's throne with confidence is because we do not have a clear understanding of who Jesus is and what he has done for us. Each of us can continually grow in our understanding of what Jesus did for us on the cross and in his resurrection. This week, take some time to study the following passages on the person and ministry of Jesus. Use the space provided to keep notes of what you learn.

PASSAGE #1: Isaiah 53:1–12

- What does this passage tell you about Jesus?

- What does this passage say Jesus did for you?

- What new understanding have you gained about Jesus's sacrifice?

PASSAGE #2: Philippians 2:1–11

- What does this passage tell you about Jesus?

- What does this passage say Jesus did for you?

- How does Paul say you are to respond to Jesus's sacrifice?

PASSAGE #3: Colossians 1:15–23

- What does this passage tell you about Jesus?

- What does this passage say Jesus did for you?

- How does Paul say you are to respond to Jesus's sacrifice?

PASSAGE #4: Hebrews 10:1–25

- What does this passage tell you about Jesus?

- What does this passage say Jesus did for you?

- How does the writer say you are to respond to what Jesus has done for you?

PASSAGE #5: Revelation 5:1–14

➤ Why is Jesus worthy to take the scroll in this passage?

➤ What do the angels say about Jesus as they praise him?

➤ What new understanding have you gained about worship from this passage?

Jesus Christ is not only our Savior but also our High Priest. He is the one who connects us to God the Father.

EXTEND AN INVITATION

We all have people in our lives who do not yet know Jesus as the Savior and leader of their lives. These people are welcome at the throne of grace. Remember, each of us had a time in our lives when we cried out to God before we were in a relationship with Jesus. At our moment of conversion, we began the conversation with God as a rebel and finished as his child. This means that God hears the prayers of sinners, rebels, and nonbelievers.

With this in mind, the next time you are talking with someone who is not a follower of Jesus and they share a deep need, let them know that you will be praying for them. As the Holy Spirit leads, you may even want to share the information from this study and invite them into a conversation about approaching God's throne of grace. If they are open, actually pray with them right in that moment, modeling the reality that the throne room of God is always open. Make your prayer simple, understandable, and bold—and pray in the name of Jesus. This simple invitation will show this person that God is ready and available at all times!

We are not coming to a throne of judgment. We are coming to a throne of grace.

JOURNAL, REFLECTIONS, AND NOTES

As you reflect on what God is teaching you through this session, use the space provided to write any key points or questions you want to bring to the next group meeting.

SESSION TWO

RECEIVING MERCY

Now is the perfect time for you to get to the throne of grace. What do you need? Mercy? It's there. You need wisdom? Or grace in some other form? You need strength? You're running out of gas and the battery is low? I'm telling you, whatever the needs are, God is able to meet every single one of them. He is faithful to answer when we come to the throne of grace.

JIM CYMBALA

OPENING REFLECTION

Justice, *mercy*, and *grace*. These are three of the biggest words in the Christian vocabulary. Though entire volumes have been written about each word, in their simplest form they can each be defined with one short sentence: "**Justice** is getting what we deserve; **mercy** is not getting the punishment we deserve; **grace** is getting good things we don't deserve."

To illustrate, imagine you are driving on a familiar road where the speed limit is clearly posted at 55 miles per hour. You are running a bit late to meet some friends, so you hit the gas pedal. You tell yourself, *I would never get a ticket for going just ten percent over the limit*, so you speed up to 61. Then you hit a downhill stretch of road, and you hardly notice the speedometer creeping up to 64. You encounter a "slow" driver, so you accelerate to 68 to pass him.

Just then . . . you see a police officer on the side of the road with a radar gun in hand—and it is pointed right at your speeding vehicle. Soon you see flashing lights in your rearview mirror, and the officer pulls you over to the side of the road. As you sit there waiting for him to step out of his car, you realize there are three ways this could play out:

1. **The officer gives you justice.** The officer gives you a ticket for the full 13 miles per hour you were over the speed limit. You have to pay the full fine—and it's a lot of money. You might even have to go to traffic school, and your insurance rates might go up. You know why—*you broke the law.* Justice can be hard!

2. **The officer gives you mercy.** The officer listens patiently as you admit you were speeding, declare that you are sorry, and promise to do your best in the future to stay within the posted speed limits. After hearing this, the officer gives you a verbal warning but does not write out a ticket. You drive off breathing a sigh of relief. Mercy is wonderful!
3. **The officer gives you grace.** The officer listens as you explain your situation. He can tell that you are stressed out and truly sorry, so in addition to *not* writing you a ticket, he offers you a word of encouragement to hang in there and have a good week. Before you drive off, he mentions that he has a stack of free car wash passes—and he gives you four deluxe coupons for a wash, wax, and interior cleaning. Grace is amazing!

This act of grace by the police officer gives us a picture of undeserved kindness, but it doesn't begin to compare to the lavish love of God offered through Jesus Christ. At the throne of grace, we discover that Christ has taken the just punishment for *all* our sins. We receive mercy and are freed from the bondage of our wrongs and rebellion. Then we receive grace upon grace upon undeserved grace.

When we understand the mercy and grace that await us every time we come to the throne of God, we will find ourselves running there as often as possible.

TALK ABOUT IT

To get things started for this second session, discuss the following questions:

- When was a time in your life (as a child, teen, or adult) that you got caught doing something you should not have been doing?
- Did you receive justice, mercy, grace, or a combination of these? Explain.

VIDEO TEACHING NOTES

Play the video segment for session two. As you watch, use the following outline to record any thoughts or concepts that stand out to you.

The powerful things that happen at the throne of grace

Why Christianity, at its core, is about the supernatural power of God

How Satan works to keep us from the throne of grace

How we receive mercy . . . every day

The difference between mercy and grace

The *key* is to get to the throne of grace

For me, prayer is just talking to God—it's that simple. Prayer is just telling God exactly how you feel. You don't have to put a mask on; you don't have to come to him whole; you don't have to come him hiding things. He already knows. I'm beginning to understand God in a more intimate way the more I talk to him and spend time with him. And it's not just in a church building. It's every day of your life, every morning, talking to him, welcoming him into your day, and just saying, "God use me; have your way in my life." —TIMINEY

GROUP DISCUSSION

Take a few minutes with your group members to discuss what you just watched and explore these concepts in Scripture.

1. Think about a time that you approached the throne of grace. How did you receive *one* of the following when you encountered the presence and power of your Maker?
    - Physical healing
    - Emotional strength
    - Relational restoration
    - Financial provision
    - Wisdom for life direction

- Hope in a hard time
- Some other provision . . .

2. Read **Hebrews 4:14–16**. In what ways can Jesus empathize with you? How should your understanding of Jesus's time on this earth cause you to have confidence in him and approach his throne of grace with bold assurance?

3. Read **Matthew 7:7–11**. What message is Jesus seeking to teach you in this passage? What does he want you to know about your heavenly Father? How much do you really embrace and believe what Jesus is teaching in these verses?

4. If God is waiting for you to *ask*, *seek*, and *knock*—what, if anything, is keeping you from drawing near him and taking him up on his offer?

5. Satan does all he can to keep God's people from coming to the throne of grace. What are some of the roadblocks and distractions the devil uses to keep people from drawing near to God in prayer? What tactics does he use to keep *you* from seeking God's face?

6. Read **2 Corinthians 10:4–6** and **Ephesians 6:10–18**. What do these passages teach about the battle you face? What do these passages say is the most effective way for you to go into battle to overcome the tactics the enemy will try to use against you?

7. Read **Psalm 32:1–7**. Think about a time you finally confessed your sins to God and cried out for mercy. How did this impact your physical, emotional, relational, or spiritual life?

8. What is a burden you are carrying right now? It could be a loved one who is far from God, something in your future that is causing you stress, a strained relationship, financial need, a physical challenge, or a spiritual battle. Share this with your group and invite them to come with you to the throne of grace to cry out to the Father.

CLOSING PRAYER

Use the prompts below to guide your group as you approach God's throne of grace together:

- Thank God for the reality that he understands your struggles and temptations, and he still warmly invites you to draw near his throne of grace.
- Pray against the lies, tactics, and efforts the enemy uses to keep you from drawing near God's throne.
- Ask for God's mercy in any and every area of your life where you find yourself wandering from his will and ways.
- Celebrate the amazing grace God freely gives you every day of your life.

Sooner or later God will permit a situation where you have nothing but him and his promises. It is at these times that you can run to the throne of his grace.

Between-Sessions Personal Study

SESSION TWO

Reflect on the content you've covered this week in *Life-Changing Prayer* by engaging in any or all of the following between-sessions activities. The time you invest will be well spent, so let God use it to draw you closer to him. At your next meeting, share with your group any key points or insights that stood out to you as you spent this time with the Lord.

PERSONAL REFLECTION

Take time in personal reflection to think about the following questions:

- Think about this statement you heard during the teaching this week: "Going to church is good, and hearing sermons is helpful, but the real spiritual action is when we draw near God at his throne of grace." Do you agree or disagree? Explain.

- What do you need to confess to God today before his throne of grace? Do you believe, with deep confidence, that he is ready to show you mercy every time you come to him with humble confession? Why or why not?

- What can you do to form a daily habit of going to the throne of grace? What life patterns will help you form a well-worn pathway to God's throne?

- How can you spend more time at the throne of grace crying out for people you love who need to experience more of God's mercy and grace?

You can come the way you are to the throne of grace, because God is the one who has invited you there.

HIDE IT IN YOUR HEART

Take some time this week to commit this simple passage of the Bible to memory:

> Then I acknowledged my sin to you and did not cover up my iniquity. I said, "I will confess my transgressions to the LORD." And you forgave the guilt of my sin. (PSALM 32:5)

As this passage sinks deep into your soul, dare to ask God, "What sin am I trying to hide, and what iniquity am I covering up?" Invite the Holy Spirit to speak loving conviction to your heart. As he shows you hidden sins, confess them one by one and prepare to experience the mercy and grace of God at his throne.

You are either going to carry your burden or give it to God. There is no other way.

REMEMBERING GOD'S GRACE

Grace means getting good and amazing things we do not deserve. Take time in the coming week to begin forming a memorial list of ways God has poured out his amazing grace in your life. Use the space provided to do the following:

- **Identify** ways God has poured out grace in your life.
- **Reflect** on how his grace has changed and impacted you.
- **Celebrate** God's good gift of grace in your life.

Identify at least three examples of God's grace through your journey of faith:

GRACE EXAMPLE #1

- *Identify:* What is one specific thing God has given you that you clearly did not deserve?

- *Reflect:* How has this gift of grace shaped, changed, or impacted your life in a positive way? Be specific.

- *Celebrate:* Write a prayer of thanks and praise for this gift of grace. Also, find a way to tell someone else during the coming week about this gift that God has given you.

GRACE EXAMPLE #2

- *Identify:* What is one specific thing God has given you that you clearly did not deserve?

- *Reflect:* How has this gift of grace shaped, changed, or impacted your life in a positive way? Be specific.

- *Celebrate:* Write a prayer of thanks and praise for this gift of grace. Also, find a way to tell someone else during the coming week about this gift that God has given you.

GRACE EXAMPLE #3

- *Identify:* What is one specific thing God has given you that you clearly did not deserve?

- *Reflect:* How has this gift of grace shaped, changed, or impacted your life in a positive way? Be specific.

- *Celebrate:* Write a prayer of thanks and praise for this gift of grace. Also, find a way to tell someone else during the coming week about this gift that God has given you.

"When you call, I will answer," is a recurrent promise in Scripture that God has given to us.

STUDY THE SUPERNATURAL

A great way to understand God's gift of grace is to read about some of the miracles that he performed in the Bible. Explore each of the following five passages and use the prompts provided to guide your study.

MIRACLE #1: God Parts the Red Sea

- Read **Exodus 14:1–31**. What events led up to the miracle described in this passage?

- What specific miracle did God perform?

- How did this miracle impact the people who experienced it?

➤ What does this miracle teach you about God?

MIRACLE #2: God Stops the Sun

➤ Read **Joshua 10:1–15**. What events led up to the miracle described in this passage?

➤ What specific miracle did God perform?

➤ How did this miracle impact the people who experienced it?

➤ What does this miracle teach you about God?

MIRACLE #3: God Shuts the Lions' Mouths

- Read **Daniel 6:1–24**. What events led up to the miracle described in this passage?

- What specific miracle did God perform?

- How did this miracle impact the people who experienced it?

- What does this miracle teach you about God?

MIRACLE #4: Jesus Feeds the Multitudes

- Read **Matthew 14:13–21**; **Mark 6:30–44**; and **John 6:1–15**. What events led up to the miracle described in these passages?

➤ What specific miracle did Jesus perform?

➤ How did this miracle impact the people who experienced it?

➤ What does this miracle teach you about God?

MIRACLE #5: Jesus Is Raised from the Dead

➤ Read **Matthew 28:1–10**; **Luke 24: 1–12**; and **John 20:1–10**. What events led up to the miracle described in these passages?

➤ What specific miracle happened here?

➤ How did this miracle impact the people who experienced it?

➤ What does this miracle teach you about God?

Come near the throne of grace today and pray to God as the one who did these miracles. Remember that he is the same yesterday, today, and forever (see Hebrews 13:8).

When we come to the throne of grace, God makes his supernatural power available to us. If we take away the supernatural, we don't have Christianity any more.

JOURNAL, REFLECTIONS, AND NOTES

As you reflect on what God is teaching you through this session, use the space provided to write any key points or questions you want to bring to the next group meeting.

SESSION THREE

Perfect Peace from God

The cure to the worry—and a cure to the paralyzing anxiety—is something called the "peace of God." Only God can give us this peace which passes all understanding. Note it's a fruit of prayer—of honest, sincere asking, worship, and praise. We can walk away from that throne of grace, from that time of prayer with God, and God says we'll walk away different while we're waiting for the answer. We will have his peace.

JIM CYMBALA

OPENING REFLECTION

Susan lives with a cloud over her life and a knot inside. She is worry-filled from the start of the day until the last restless second before she falls asleep. When the alarm rings in the morning, her mind begins to churn. *Too much needs to be done . . .* she can already feel the stress. Potential people conflict is ahead. She imagines the worst, and a slight pain jabs at her stomach. Family tensions await her at the breakfast table. She wishes she could just stay in bed.

She presses forward after finally forcing herself to take a shower and get dressed. All day long she expects the worst, worries endlessly, and lets the potential for problems dominate her thoughts. By the time she arrives home she is exhausted, wound up, and longing to go to bed. Sadly, she can't. There are things to do and texts and emails to answer.

By the time she allows herself a half hour to "veg out" in front of the TV, she is ready to lay in bed and worry about what went wrong today and what tough things she might face tomorrow. The jab in her stomach has now become a dull burning pain. She wonders, *Do I have an ulcer? Is it even possible for a seventh grader to worry so much that she would get an ulcer?* Before Susan falls asleep, she whispers to herself, *If anyone could have an ulcer at twelve years old, it would be me!*

In our worry-filled world, even children are facing the reality that peace is hard to find. Kids hardly get a chance to be kids, and many adults spend much of their time and energy on the management of anxiety and worry. God has a better plan for his children of all ages. He offers peace no matter what we face in any season of our lives.

TALK ABOUT IT

To get things started for this third session, discuss one *of the following questions:*

- Think about a time when worry got its hooks into your heart and mind. How did this worry manifest itself? How did it affect your life?
- If you know people who are prone to worry, how are their lives, relationships, and even their health damaged by the presence of ongoing anxiety?

VIDEO TEACHING NOTES

Play the video segment for session three. As you watch, use the following outline to record any thoughts or concepts that stand out to you.

What worry does to us

Our response to God's command to not worry about a single thing

Why worry is actually a sin

The prescription to worry . . .

Lift up supplication

Mix in thanksgiving

What it means to have the peace of God

How we seek peace at the throne of grace

Even when I have my days or I'm just sad, I know God is going to get me through. And he does. I can go to Jesus and he gets me. And having seen how he's helped me wake up every day and just keep going and not give up—that's been him. So, I'm confident there's nothing too hard for him. I know whatever the rest of my life looks like, he knows. I don't know, but he's going to be with me. He's going to help me through whatever those challenges are. He answered me in my time of trouble. In my time of devastation, he answered me.

—CHRYSTAL

GROUP DISCUSSION

Take a few minutes with your group members to discuss what you just watched and explore these concepts in Scripture.

1. How has worry become a normal and acceptable part of our world and culture?

2. Read **Philippians 4:4–7**. What are some of the attitudes that the apostle Paul talks about in this passage? How should these attitudes be apparent in the life of a committed and growing Jesus follower?

3. What is the relationship between prayer and peace? According to Philippians 4:4–7, what will the peace of God do when it is unleashed in a person's life?

4. *Supplication* is speaking to God about specific needs and asking for his intervention, provision, and help. Why is it important to tell God about what is on your heart—even when you are certain he already knows?

5. Why is it critical to sprinkle thanksgiving throughout your prayers of supplication? What message are you sending God and others when all you do is ask of God and neglect to lift up honest and joyful thanksgiving?

6. Think about a time you came to the throne of grace filled with worry and anxiety and walked away filled with peace. How did this new attitude impact your life as you continued to face the situation that was bringing you anxiety?

7. Your peace is not based on your situation or what is happening around you but is rooted in the God who promises his peace no matter what you face. How can you grow in your assurance that God is on the throne, even when you go through hard times?

8. What is one area of life (yours or a person you care about) that you are worrying about? How can your group members join you at the throne of grace as you cry out to God about this deep need?

CLOSING PRAYER

Use the prompts below to guide your group as you approach God's throne of grace together:

- Confess the times and situations in which you tend to grow worried rather than seek the peace of God.
- Ask the Holy Spirit to help you turn to God in prayer quickly and passionately when you feel worry growing in your heart.
- Bring any of your group members before the throne of grace and ask God to help them grow in peace as they pray more and worry less.
- Thank God for how he has been faithful to you in the past. Acknowledge that his past work in your life assures you that he will be faithful in the future.

If there is any testimony we have as Christians in the world today, it is that we have the peace of God.

Between-Sessions Personal Study

SESSION THREE

Reflect on the content you've covered this week in *Life-Changing Prayer* by engaging in any or all of the following between-sessions activities. The time you invest will be well spent, so let God use it to draw you closer to him. At your next meeting, share with your group any key points or insights that stood out to you as you spent this time with the Lord.

PERSONAL REFLECTION

Take time in personal reflection to think about the following questions:

- What are some of the ways you might try to justify or excuse worry in your life? How will you refuse to entertain these lies in the future?

- How do you respond to the idea that *worry is sin*? Why do believers in Christ tend to resist saying this and believing it?

- What situations trigger worry most quickly in your heart? How can you run to the throne of grace the next time you face these situations instead of growing anxious?

- How has God surprised you with his peace when you've come near his throne of grace? What can you learn from past experiences of God's peace that passes understanding?

God says, "That hurts me, that grieves me, when my children worry." And what does worry change, anyway? In your life . . . worry changes nothing.

MY SINGLE THING

The New Testament was written in Greek, and sometimes the original language carries subtle meanings that can be missed with a casual reading. For instance, in Philippians 4:6 we read, "Do not be anxious about anything." But another way to read this passage is, "Don't worry, not even about a single thing." This could cause us to consider what our "single thing" might be.

As we grow mature in faith, we still battle with sin. Worry is sin—and many of us often don't take it as seriously as we should. We tend to have a "single thing" that seems to stay locked in our heart and life. Though we might be avoiding many sources of worry, there can be a hidden area we just can't seem to stop being anxious about.

Today, consider what is your "single thing"—that one area in life you just can't seem to help but worry about. Be honest as you write about this situation.

- My "single thing":

- What seems to trigger my worry and send me down the path of anxiety:

- How I can turn to God and approach his throne of grace with confidence when I sense one of these triggers:

What helps faith grow is remembering how God has already been good in our lives—and then giving him thanks for it.

HIDE IT IN YOUR HEART

Take time this week to commit this passage of the Bible to memory:

> Do not be anxious about anything, but in every situation, by prayer and petition, with thanksgiving, present your requests to God. And the peace of God, which transcends all understanding, will guard your hearts and your minds in Christ Jesus. (PHILIPPIANS 4:6-7)

Recite this passage each time you find your heart racing or your mind wandering toward the world of worry. Keep it on a card or save it as a note in your phone. Read it again and again until you have it hidden in your heart, and begin praying. As you do, you will find the peace of Christ at the throne of grace.

The cure to anxiety is the peace that passes all understanding.

THANKSGIVING SPICE

It is always good to "spice up" your prayer life up with thanksgiving. When you sprinkle in thanks, the rest of your prayers take on a more hopeful and faith-filled flavor. Today, make a list of things for which you are thankful that you can sprinkle into your prayer times.

➤ Things God has done for me:

- Spiritual blessings God has poured out on me:

- Material resources God has put in my care:

- Ways God has rescued me and delivered me in the past:

- Wonderful people God has placed in my life:

As you pray, sprinkle these thanks, and others, into your prayers of need and supplication.

How can we expect answers for new grace when we haven't thanked God for what he has already done?

JOURNAL, REFLECTIONS, AND NOTES

As you reflect on what God is teaching you through this session, use the space provided to write any key points or questions you want to bring to the next group meeting.

SESSION FOUR

PRAYING WITH FAITH

It is impossible for our prayers to be at their greatest power if we do not recognize the Holy Spirit and depend on his help. One of the many ways the Holy Spirit helps us is in this vital matter of prayer. He was sent to take the Word of God and create faith in our hearts so we're not just praying to the wind and hoping God will answer—but we're praying with faith in our hearts. The Word of God is made real by the Holy Spirit to bring faith as we pray.

JIM CYMBALA

OPENING REFLECTION

Karl grew up in a strict Protestant home. His family went to church Sunday morning, Sunday evening, and midweek for catechism classes. He prayed before every meal . . . even in public places. His meal prayer was exactly what he heard his father pray every evening at the dinner table as he grew up: "Lord, thank you for this food and drink. We are truly thankful for your bounteous provision. Bless this food to our bodies that we might serve you this day. God bless our family, our friends, and our nation. In Jesus's name, Amen." If you asked Karl whether he prayed, he would say with honesty, "Every day, three times a day!"

Julia grew up in a religious environment. Her grandmother was a devout Catholic who talked about her faith all the time. Julia's father and mother took the family to church on the big holidays, and they always referred to themselves as "good Catholics." Julia grew up believing it was important to communicate with God, so she prayed the Rosary when she felt a need to talk with God. She could say the "Hail Mary" and the "Lord's Prayer" from memory. If you asked Julia, "Do you pray?" she would confidently say, "Yes, whenever I need to!"

Shannon grew up with no church, no faith, and no religious background. No one in her immediate family seemed to even think about spiritual things. Shannon, on the other hand, wondered about God, pondered if there is life after death, and thought about things like angels, heaven, and her own soul. She was not sure if God existed, but she hoped there was a God out there who loved her. From her youngest days, she talked to God throughout her day. Nothing fancy—she just told God what she was feeling, shared her fears, and thanked him for helping her each day. If you asked Shannon if she prayed, she would be a little shy about it, but she would say, "I think so. I talk to God all the time, but I am not completely sure he hears me."

What is the *right* way to pray? How do we learn to pray? Even Jesus's disciples felt they had a lot to learn about prayer, so they asked Christ to teach them how to pray better. Even long-term and mature followers of Jesus can keep growing in their understanding and practice of prayer. No matter how long you have been seeking to communicate with God in prayer, one of the most important things you can do is learn to pray with bold and confident faith.

TALK ABOUT IT

To get things started for this fourth session, discuss one of the following questions:

- Who modeled or taught you how to pray? What did they teach you about this important part of a life of faith?
- What is one of your favorite Bible verses about prayer? Why is this verse meaningful? How does it help you know how to pray?

VIDEO TEACHING NOTES

Play the video segment for session four. As you watch, use the following outline to record any thoughts or concepts that stand out to you.

When we don't know how to pray as we should

The relationship between prayer and the Holy Spirit

How the Holy Spirit helps us pray and empowers our prayers

How the Spirit makes God's Word come alive as we pray

How the Holy Spirit brings fervency to our prayers

The ways the Holy Spirit gives utterance to things we can't express without his help

I think it's not only during the really tumultuous times or a time of tribulation that God answers prayer. We have a real, everyday, living faith, and we can call on him at any point, at any time in our lives, for whatever the situation may be. That's how close he is—he's as close as the mention of his name. He loves us and wants to rescue us and help us all the time. —PAM

GROUP DISCUSSION

Take a few minutes with your group members to discuss what you just watched and explore these concepts in Scripture.

1. How would you describe the relationship between the Holy Spirit and prayer? How do your prayers change when the Spirit is present? What impact does it have on your prayers if the Holy Spirit is not present and at work?

2. Read **Romans 8:26–27**. What does Paul mean when he says, "We do not know what we ought to pray for"? What is an aspect of prayer you misunderstood when you were younger in the faith? What helped you gain a more biblical understanding?

3. Christianity without the presence of the Holy Spirit is powerless. What are some signs that might indicate you are living the Christian life in your own power and not the power of the Holy Spirit?

4. Read **1 Corinthians 2:2–5**. Discuss how the presence and power of the Holy Spirit impact any *one* of the following:
   - The preaching of God's Word
   - Sharing the message of Jesus when you witness to others
   - Your efforts to live for Jesus
   - Your efforts to resist sin and temptation
   - The direction and content of your prayers
   - The power and impact of your prayers

5. How does the Holy Spirit fill you with passion, fervor, and energy as you invite him to lead you in prayer? When was a time you specifically felt the Holy Spirit guiding you in prayer? How did the Spirit of God fill that prayer with passion?

6. The Bible provides us with instruction for living, but it does not always tell us specifically what to do—who we should marry, how much we should give, what career path to take. In these instances, the Holy Spirit will guide and direct us into the will of our heavenly Father. When was a time in your life that you asked God for direction on a specific life decision (big or small)? How did the Holy Spirit guide and lead you?

7. Why is it so important to invite the Holy Spirit to speak, direct, lead, and guide your life *each day*? Why is it necessary to ask specific and pointed questions of the Holy Spirit? Why should you expect equally clear and detailed answers?

8. What is one area of your life in which you need to seek the Holy Spirit for a specific answer? How can your group members approach the throne of grace with you today and cry out for God's clear answer and leading in this particular area?

CLOSING PRAYER

Use the prompts below to guide your group as you approach God's throne of grace together:

- Thank God for the people who taught you to pray and modeled how to seek God's face and draw near to the throne of grace.
- Invite the Holy Spirit to teach you more and more ways to express yourself in prayer—even if they stretch you a bit.
- Thank the Holy Spirit for answering specific prayers in your past in a way that gives you confidence that he will lead you in the future.
- Ask the Holy Spirit to continue to grow your fervor and passion as you go deeper in prayer.
- Lift up a specific area of your life where you need direction or clear leading from the Spirit. Ask with bold confidence for the Spirit to speak to you and guide you.

The capacity to receive from God is always related to desire and fervency. As we pray with the Holy Spirit's help, we pray fervently, "I am intent on hearing an answer from you."

Between-Sessions Personal Study

SESSION FOUR

Reflect on the content you've covered this week in *Life-Changing Prayer* by engaging in any or all of the following between-sessions activities. The time you invest will be well spent, so let God use it to draw you closer to him. At your next meeting, share with your group any key points or insights that stood out to you as you spent this time with the Lord.

PERSONAL REFLECTION

Take time in personal reflection to think about the following questions:

- Are there things you were taught about prayer that are not accurate or have even gotten in the way of you praying with passion and power? (Invite the Holy Spirit to show you where you need to grow in your prayer life.)

- Think about some aspect of prayer that you feel you still don't fully understand. What are ways you could find answers to your questions about prayer? How could you go deeper in your understanding of prayer and your personal engagement in it?

- How have you experienced the Holy Spirit moving and speaking when you open the Bible and read what he inspired more than two thousand years ago? When was a time you read the Bible and clearly experienced the Holy Spirit teaching, inspiring, or convicting you?

- What are some ways you could express yourself in prayer to God that would be new and fresh and would unleash your heart to connect more fully with the heart of God?

The Holy Spirit makes our prayers heartfelt—from our heart to God's heart.

SPRINGBOARD PRAYERS

God did not give you the prayers in the Bible to mindlessly repeat or recite—to just commit to memory and lift up with no heart or passion. When Jesus taught his followers to pray in the Sermon on the Mount, he was clear that they were not to just mindlessly babble and repeat empty words. The words Jesus taught his followers are meant to be a springboard to launch you into the endless and refreshing waters of prayer. With this in mind, study the following two prayers of Jesus. Identify the key themes and directions of Jesus in his prayer, and then use these to guide your own prayers as the Holy Spirit leads.

PRAYER #1: The Lord's Prayer (Matthew 6:9–13)

> Our Father in heaven,
> hallowed be your name,
> your kingdom come,
> your will be done,
>   on earth as it is in heaven.
> Give us today our daily bread.
> And forgive us our debts,
>   as we also have forgiven our debtors.
> And lead us not into temptation,
>   but deliver us from the evil one.

➤ Some of the key themes and directions in Jesus's prayer:

➤ How these themes can springboard you into new places in prayer:

PRAYER #2: Jesus's High Priestly Prayer (John 17:1–26)

Father, the hour has come. Glorify your Son, that your Son may glorify you. For you granted him authority over all people that he might give eternal life to all those you have given him. Now this is eternal life: that they know you, the only true God, and Jesus Christ, whom you have sent. I have brought you glory on earth by finishing the work you gave me to do. And now, Father, glorify me in your presence with the glory I had with you before the world began.

I have revealed you to those whom you gave me out of the world. They were yours; you gave them to me and they have obeyed your word. Now they know that everything you have given me comes from you. For I gave them the words you gave me and they accepted them. They knew with certainty that I came from you, and they believed that you sent me. I pray for them. I am not praying for the world, but for those you have given me, for they are yours. All I have is yours, and all you have is mine. And glory has come to me through them. I will remain in the world no longer, but they are still in the world, and I am coming to you. Holy Father, protect them by the power of your name, the name you gave me, so that they may be one as we are one. While I was with them, I protected them and kept them safe by that name you gave me. None has been lost except the one doomed to destruction so that Scripture would be fulfilled.

I am coming to you now, but I say these things while I am still in the world, so that they may have the full measure of my joy within them. I have given them your word and the world has hated them, for they are not of the world any more than I am of the world. My prayer is not that you take them out of the world but that you protect them from the evil one. They are not of the world, even as I am not of it. Sanctify them by the truth; your word is truth. As you sent me into the world, I have sent them into the world. For them I sanctify myself, that they too may be truly sanctified.

My prayer is not for them alone. I pray also for those who will believe in me through their message, that all of them may be one, Father, just as you are in me and I am in you. May they also be in us so that the world may believe that you have sent me. I have given them the glory that you gave me, that they may be one as we are one—I in them and you in me—so that they may be brought to complete unity. Then the world will know that you sent me and have loved them even as you have loved me.

Father, I want those you have given me to be with me where I am, and to see my glory, the glory you have given me because you loved me before the creation of the world.

Righteous Father, though the world does not know you, I know you, and they know that you have sent me. I have made you known to them, and will continue to make you known in order that the love you have for me may be in them and that I myself may be in them.

➤ Some of the key themes and directions in Jesus's prayer:

➤ How these themes can springboard you into new places in prayer:

As we go to prayer, we should not only think of the promises and the beauty of the promise of the throne of grace, but we should say, "Holy Spirit, help us to pray."

LETTING THE PSALMS PRAY FOR YOU

It has been said the Bible teaches us to pray, but the psalms pray *for* us. So today, take some time to read and reflect on the following psalms and how each can guide you in your own prayers. Let the heart of the psalms become your heart. Remember, the Holy Spirit breathed and inspired every word of the Bible. As you pray the words of each psalm and make these words your prayer, you will be praying the Spirit-uttered words of God!

PSALM #1: Psalm 8:1–9

LORD, our Lord,
 how majestic is your name in all the earth!
You have set your glory
 in the heavens.
Through the praise of children and infants
 you have established a stronghold against your enemies,
 to silence the foe and the avenger.

When I consider your heavens,
the work of your fingers,
the moon and the stars,
which you have set in place,
what is mankind that you are mindful of them,
human beings that you care for them?
You have made them a little lower than the angels
and crowned them with glory and honor.
You made them rulers over the works of your hands;
you put everything under their feet:
all flocks and herds,
and the animals of the wild,
the birds in the sky,
and the fish in the sea,
all that swim the paths of the seas.
LORD, our Lord,
how majestic is your name in all the earth!

➤ How this psalm leads you to pray:

PSALM #2: Psalm 9:1–20

I will give thanks to you, LORD, with all my heart;
I will tell of all your wonderful deeds.
I will be glad and rejoice in you;
I will sing the praises of your name, O Most High.
My enemies turn back;
they stumble and perish before you.

For you have upheld my right and my cause,
    sitting enthroned as the righteous judge.
You have rebuked the nations and destroyed the wicked;
    you have blotted out their name for ever and ever.
Endless ruin has overtaken my enemies,
    you have uprooted their cities;
    even the memory of them has perished.
The LORD reigns forever;
    he has established his throne for judgment.
He rules the world in righteousness
    and judges the peoples with equity.
The LORD is a refuge for the oppressed,
    a stronghold in times of trouble.
Those who know your name trust in you,
    for you, LORD, have never forsaken those who seek you.
Sing the praises of the LORD, enthroned in Zion;
    proclaim among the nations what he has done.
For he who avenges blood remembers;
    he does not ignore the cries of the afflicted.
LORD, see how my enemies persecute me!
    Have mercy and lift me up from the gates of death,
that I may declare your praises
    in the gates of Daughter Zion,
    and there rejoice in your salvation.
The nations have fallen into the pit they have dug;
    their feet are caught in the net they have hidden.
The LORD is known by his acts of justice;
    the wicked are ensnared by the work of their hands.
The wicked go down to the realm of the dead,
    all the nations that forget God.
But God will never forget the needy;
    the hope of the afflicted will never perish.
Arise, LORD, do not let mortals triumph;

let the nations be judged in your presence.
Strike them with terror, LORD;
let the nations know they are only mortal.

➤ How this psalm leads you to pray:

PSALM #3: Psalm 23:1–6

The LORD is my shepherd, I lack nothing.
He makes me lie down in green pastures,
he leads me beside quiet waters,
he refreshes my soul.
He guides me along the right paths
for his name's sake.
Even though I walk
through the darkest valley,
I will fear no evil,
for you are with me;
your rod and your staff,
they comfort me.
You prepare a table before me
in the presence of my enemies.
You anoint my head with oil;
my cup overflows.
Surely your goodness and love will follow me
all the days of my life,
and I will dwell in the house of the LORD
forever.

➤ How this psalm leads you to pray:

Neat little compact prayers with introductions and endings are nowhere found in Scripture.

EXPANDING YOUR PRAYER VOCABULARY

Take thirty minutes today to go somewhere private where you can be alone with God. See if you can find at least three ways to express your innermost thoughts (for example: praise, thanks, need, sorrow, honor) to the Lord . . . without using words. Stretch yourself. Groans can be prayer. Tears speak to the heart of God. Sounds of joy delight God's heart. Be creative, and let God stretch your ability to pray. Use the space provided below and on the next two pages to record three new ways you sought to communicate with God and how this deepened your prayers or expanded your communication horizons.

New Way of Prayer #1: ______________________________

➤ How this helped express what was in your heart:

- How you felt as you were praying without words in this unique way:

NEW WAY OF PRAYER #2: ______________________

- How this helped express what was in your heart:

- How you felt as you were praying without words in this unique way:

NEW WAY OF PRAYER #3: ______________________

- How this helped express what was in your heart:

- How you felt as you were praying without words in this unique way:

God provides for us when we depend on the Holy Spirit—both in the praying and the doing according to his will.

JOURNAL, REFLECTIONS, AND NOTES

As you reflect on what God is teaching you through this session, use the space provided to write any key points or questions you want to bring to the next group meeting.

SESSION FIVE

God Brings the Answer

There is no stopping the power of prayer. There's no stopping God from answering our prayers as our hearts reach up to him and we pray according to the Word of God. We can't be discouraged by anything we're facing today, because we walk by faith, not by sight. It doesn't matter what we see right now—for what we see is not what God sees. We have to hold on to God and say, "We're not letting you go until we see your promises fulfilled in our lives, our families, and our churches." There's no telling what God can do when his people pray.

JIM CYMBALA

OPENING REFLECTION

Have you ever tried to imagine what prayer must be like from God's perspective? Millions of voices crying out at the same time. Hearts lifted up. Every language imaginable. Try to envision what God hears.

A little German girl raised in the Lutheran Church in Berlin is asking God to bring her father home. He has been gone so long, and she misses him. "God, my heavenly Father, bring my papa home so my mother will not cry at night."

An elderly Ethiopian couple holds hands and prays for rain, for crops, for provision, and for hope. Tears of sincere need flow down their faces. "Creator God, you made the heavens and the earth. You love your people. In the name of Jesus, provide bread for our family. This is all we ask: daily bread and water."

A single mother in El Salvador stands in her one-room home and looks at her three children all sharing the same bed. Her prayer is whispered with hands stretched over her sleeping children. "God of mercy and grace, protect my children from gangs and drugs. Let them love Jesus all the days of their life. Lord Jesus, send angels to protect them when they are in my home and even more when they are out of my sight."

A cynical agnostic businessman in Cincinnati gets in his BMW after a twelve-hour workday and rests his head on the steering wheel. "I am so tired . . . I don't know if I can keep up this pace. Higher Power of the Universe, God . . . if someone is out there, give me a sign. Help! I have not told anyone else, not even my wife, but I am at the end of my rope. Amen, or whatever you say to end this . . . I guess you would call it . . . prayer."

People from every tongue, tribe, political party, economic background, nation, age group, and walk of life cry out to God. Does he really hear? Does he answer? Does he care? Does he have the time to be interested, the power to help, and the compassion to draw near?

The truth is that God hears *every* prayer—even prayers of the most hardened sinner. He hears the whispered and desperate prayers of atheists. He hears the memorized prayers of "religious" people who go through the motions but forget what their memorized prayers really mean. He hears children who pray for food to survive or to get a puppy on their birthday.

If we are going to grow in prayer, we must recognize that God is far more attentive than we realize and that he delights in answering our prayers.

TALK ABOUT IT

To get things started for this fifth session, discuss one *of the following questions:*

- When you think about God hearing (and caring about) all the prayers of all people at the same time, what does this tell you about his power, character, and heart?
- When God answers our prayers, what do you think motivates him to hear, care, and respond to us?

VIDEO TEACHING NOTES

Play the video segment for session five. As you watch, use the following outline to record any thoughts or concepts that stand out to you.

Why faith is critical when it comes to prayer

How we are to pray with childlike faith

How to grow our faith . . . by meditating daily on the Word of God

Why emotions are the biggest enemy of faith in our prayer life

What we learn about prayer from the story of Cornelius in Acts 10

Why we must hold on to God until he fulfills his promise

When you've lost everything, sometimes you wonder, *Does God see? Does God care? Does he want to help with the things that life can hand us?* When I think about my experience in Ethiopia, it was certainly a reminder to me that God does see, and does care, and does want to be able to meet us in our places of brokenness. He wants to encourage us and remind us that he does love us. He wants us to call on him, and he wants us to trust him for the things that are so challenging in this life. —BRIAN

GROUP DISCUSSION

Take a few minutes with your group members to discuss what you just watched and explore these concepts in Scripture.

1. Think about a time you sought God with all your heart and came to the throne of grace diligently. How did God reward you? What benefits did you receive from him? (Remember that God rewards his children in a wide variety of ways.)

2. Read **James 5:13–16**. James is clear in stating that when we are in trouble, we should pray—almost as a reflexive response. What are some things you tend to do before you pray whenever you hit hard times, face challenges, or experience pain? Why is moving directly to prayer before any of these actions the wisest and most effective course?

3. Why does James say we are to pray for those who are sick? Why is it important to invite the leaders of the church into this experience of asking for divine healing? When was a time you saw God heal someone in response to prayer?

4. Read **Hebrews 11:5–6**. Why does the author state that "without faith it is impossible to please God"? How is faith in Jesus essential for you to truly please God? How does faith in God's presence and power impact the way he answers your prayers?

5. The author of Hebrews teaches that God "rewards those who earnestly seek him" (11:6). What does it look like to earnestly seek God in prayer? What are ways you can pursue God with greater passion and diligence?

6. Read **Matthew 18:1–3**. What does *childlike* faith look like? What are some ways that children trust God and have confidence in him that we adults can emulate?

7. How can emotions get in the way of faith? What are some ways you can tame your emotional responses and grow your faith by trusting the steadfastness of God more than the inconsistency of your emotions?

8. There are many ways to go deeper in our prayer life and in faith. What are some practical ways you and your group members can do each of the following?
   - Spend more time praying
   - Pray with bolder faith
   - Ask more of God in prayer
   - Expect more from God in response to prayer

CLOSING PRAYER

Use the prompts below to guide your group as you approach God's throne of grace together:

- Thank God for hearing every prayer you have ever lifted up—even prayers you groaned, prayers you have forgotten, and prayers offered before you truly believed in him.
- Ask God to deepen your faith and grow your trust that he hears you every time you talk to him and longs to answer your prayers.
- Pray that God will receive glory every time he answers a prayer. Ask the Holy Spirit to give you opportunities to share stories of answered prayer so others will also give God the praise.
- Ask God to help you meditate on his Word until it shapes your prayers.
- Confess where your emotions get in the way of you trusting God as you pray. Ask God to give you confidence in his faithfulness no matter what your emotions are telling you.

"Is anybody in trouble? Let him pray!" Whatever the trouble is, we have the promise that God is the one who is going to bring the answer.

Between-Sessions Personal Study

SESSION FIVE

Reflect on the content you've covered this week in *Life-Changing Prayer* by engaging in any or all of the following between-sessions activities. The time you invest will be well spent, so let God use it to draw you closer to him. At your next meeting, share with your group any key points or insights that stood out to you as you spent this time with the Lord.

PERSONAL REFLECTION

Take time in personal reflection to think about the following questions:

- How has reading the Bible and letting the Scriptures become part of your thinking shaped and impacted your prayer life? What is one specific passage in the Bible that has really guided your prayers and deepened your faith?

- What lies has the enemy told you about God's love, his interest in your prayers, or his desire to answer your prayers? How can the truth of the Bible overcome these lies?

- How can you encourage others to pray more—perhaps even those who are not yet followers of Jesus?

- What can you do to increase in childlike faith and trust that God answers your prayers?

If you want to be strong in prayer, be in the Word of God each day.

HISTORY LEADS TO CONFIDENCE

When you look back at your life and see how God has answered so many prayers, it gives you confidence that he will continue to be faithful and answer your prayers as you move forward. He is the same yesterday, today, and forever! Today, do a brief historical survey of your life to remember God's powerful and faithful answers to prayers you have lifted up in the past. Then use the spaces provided to record, reflect, and rejoice! (Note: If you are younger and the later sections don't apply to you, just record more prayers that God answered in your current stage of life.)

STAGE #1: Childhood

- List one prayer that God answered during your childhood days:

- Write a short reflection on how God answered this prayer:

- Write a prayer of praise, rejoicing in God's faithfulness to you in that season of life:

STAGE #2: Young Adult

➤ List one prayer that God answered during your young adult days:

➤ Write a short reflection on how God answered this prayer:

➤ Write a prayer of praise, rejoicing in God's faithfulness to you in that season of life:

STAGE #3: Adult

➤ List one prayer that God answered during your 30s, 40s, 50s, or beyond:

➤ Write a short reflection on how God answered this prayer:

➤ Write a prayer of praise, rejoicing in God's faithfulness to you in that season of life:

Sometimes we have little faith, so we make little prayers . . . and get little answers.

HIDE IT IN YOUR HEART

The Bible says that the enemy of your soul is a liar and the father of lies (see John 8:44). He breathes lies at all times, and you need to battle his lies with God's truth. Today, take time to meditate on (and even memorize) the following passages to help you stand strong when the lies of the enemy are coming your way:

> You, dear children, are from God and have overcome them, because the one who is in you is greater than the one who is in the world. (1 JOHN 4:4)

> The devil . . . was a murderer from the beginning, not holding to the truth, for there is no truth in him. When he lies, he speaks his native language, for he is a liar and the father of lies. (JOHN 8:44)

> Finally, be strong in the Lord and in his mighty power. Put on the full armor of God, so that you can take your stand against the devil's schemes. For our struggle is not against flesh and blood, but against the rulers, against the authorities, against the powers of this dark world and against the spiritual forces of evil in the heavenly realms. Therefore put on the full armor of God, so that when the day of evil comes, you may be able to stand your ground, and after you have done everything, to stand. (EPHESIANS 6:10-13)

If we know the promises of God, we can pray with faith, "God, do as you promised."

PRAYING FOR YOUR WORLD

At the end of the day, no nation will have revival, be fruitful, and honor God because its people elected the right person to office. Political parties will never transform a country and make it a shining reflection of God's love and truth. Only the King of Kings and Lord of Lords can change human hearts, transform cultures, and bring the revival our world needs. With this in mind, consider praying for your country in the following ways:

- *Pray for your national leaders:* Once a week, devote time to praying for your local, state, and national leaders. Find a list of their names by doing a search on the internet; write down three to five names; and pray for them every day this week (no matter what political party they represent). As you pray for these individuals, ask for God to move in your city, state, and nation in powerful ways. Invite him to work through these leaders, whether they know him or not.
- *Pray for your civic leaders:* As you walk and drive around your community, pray for your civic leaders and community servants. When you pass the post office, pray for those who work there. When you drive by a public school, pray for the teachers. When you see a police officer or fire fighter, ask God to protect and use them. Cover those who serve in your community with prayer.
- *Pray for your community:* Declare God as the king and ruler of your neighborhood, community, state, and nation. Take time in prayer to recognize his sovereignty, and offer every part of your world to him. Begin with your own heart and home, and then move out into your neighborhood and beyond.

God will supply our needs and answer our prayers so that his name will be glorified. He is always listening to the prayers of his people.

JOURNAL, REFLECTIONS, AND NOTES

As you reflect on what God is teaching you through this session, use the space provided to write any key points or questions you want to bring to the next group meeting.

SESSION SIX

The Church That Prays Together

There's a saying that "the church that prays together stays together." And it's true. You can't pray sincerely with a person and then, in a short period of time, be burying them in an avalanche of gossip and slander. When we pray with one another, our hearts become tender. We realize how much we mutually need God and how we mutually need to encourage each other. So let's love one another, and as we love one another, let's gather together and pray together. When we do, there's no telling what God might do.

JIM CYMBALA

OPENING REFLECTION

Third Street Church had been struggling with their budget for ten years. They simply could not afford to pay the pastor, keep up the building, support three missionaries out in the field, and pay the utilities. The pastor had tried everything to improve the situation.

He had hired a church fundraising company to do an extensive capital campaign. He had preached a three-week series on generosity and tithing. He had appealed to denominational headquarters for financial support and applied for a couple of grants. He had pressured the congregation with sermons and emails about the plight of the church. He had tried to inspire them with examples of people who had given sacrificially.

In a desperate effort to break through to his congregational members, the pastor had even threatened to save them money by packing up and moving to serve another congregation. Now, he was at the end of his rope. He had tried—and failed—at every attempt to move the church forward and unleash the finances needed for their ministry.

Well, *almost* every attempt.

One day, the pastor had a radical idea. What if he began his days on his knees seeking God rather than pacing his office worrying? What if the board meetings were not focused on problem solving but on spending time before the throne of grace together? What if he called the entire congregation to enter a season of prayer for the power of the Holy Spirit to invade their church, their hearts, and their lives? What if every ministry wove prayer into its gathering . . . for the work, power, and inbreaking of God?

After ten years of trying everything else, the pastor decided to lead his congregation to the throne of grace!

TALK ABOUT IT

To get things started for this final session, discuss one *of the following questions:*

- Why do you think we often look at prayer as a last-ditch effort and final action rather than the very first thing we should do?
- When have you seen a church or ministry turn around because its members chose to seek God and pray together?

VIDEO TEACHING NOTES

Play the video segment for session six. As you watch, use the following outline to record any thoughts or concepts that stand out to you.

What we would see and learn if we went back to the New Testament church

The elements of life we find in the New Testament church:

The apostles' teaching (biblical learning)

Fellowship (family love)

Breaking of bread (meals in homes and communion)

Prayer (of all sorts)

Why God's people should gather to pray

How prayer brings resources from heaven

What it means to *build* the church on prayer

How disunity hinders prayer and grieves the Holy Spirit

I believe God is waiting to be invited into the life of every congregation, to shape that congregation, to infuse his life in that congregation, to challenge that congregation for transformation, and to be transformative in the community, if that congregation will begin to call on God. Not just lip service to prayer, but really have an effective corporate expression of prayer. —ALEC

GROUP DISCUSSION

Take a few minutes with your group members to discuss what you just watched and explore these concepts in Scripture.

1. If you could go back to the first century and observe the church for thirty days, what do you think you would notice that is different from the church today? Why do you think these differences have developed over time?

2. Read **Acts 2:42–47**. How do you see the four key elements of church life—teaching God's Word, fellowship, breaking of bread, and prayers—modeled in the early church? How did God bless their faithfulness?

3. Which of these practices do you see in your church today? What are specific ways you could go deeper into each of these practices as a church? How could you better develop each of these in your small-group community?

4. Read **Acts 12:1–7**. How could this church have responded to Peter's arrest other than praying? Why was prayer the first and only option for them? What happened in direct response to their prayers?

5. When we pray, God pours out the resources of heaven. What are some of the things God gives, does, and unleashes when his people pray?

6. Disunity breaks the heart of God, quenches the Holy Spirit, and keeps the people of God from praying. How does slander, gossip, unforgiveness, negative talk, and complaining creep into the life of the local church? What can be done to guard against these sources of disunity and keep them from taking root?

7. Read **Philippians 2:2–4**. When we strive for peace and unity, we create an environment in which the Spirit flows and prayer becomes a natural part of our community life. What are some ways you can grow and develop in love, humility, forgiveness, mutual respect, and mercy? How would this positively affect your church and small group?

8. Are you currently experiencing disunity with another Christian or a group of Jesus followers? If so, what can you do to seek unity and move back to being able to pray with this person or group of people? How can your group members pray for you and keep you accountable to seek restoration and peace?

CLOSING PRAYER

Use the prompts below to guide your group as you approach God's throne of grace together:

- Confess to God the ways you have based your understanding of the church on traditions rather than on the model of the biblical church.
- Pray for your church to embrace prayer as a core and central part of all you do as a community of faith.
- Thank God for specific answers to prayer your local church has experienced through their history and in recent days.
- Pray against the prayer-stopping and Spirit-quenching behaviors that can damage a local church.
- Ask God to unleash the practices and behaviors that propel a church forward in unity and prayer.

The greatest churches in the history of the Christian era have been churches founded on prayer.

Final Personal Study

SESSION SIX

Reflect on the content you've covered during this final week in *Life-Changing Prayer* by engaging in any or all of the following activities. The time you invest will be well spent, so let God use it to draw you closer to him. In the coming days, be sure to share with your group leader or group members any key points or insights that stood out to you.

PERSONAL REFLECTION

Take time in personal reflection to think about the following questions:

- What are your patterns and habits when it comes to church? Which ones are biblical and which ones are simply following personal, family, or church traditions? How can you develop more biblical patterns in your relationship to the local church?

- If prayer is the barometer of your spiritual life and the health of a church, how would you rate the health of your own spiritual life and that of the church you attend?

- What are some ways you have seen God glorified in your life, your family, and your church because you have prayed and God has answered?

- What hindrances do you have to prayer in your life? What can you do to remove them?

Prayer is about the glory of God, so we will have a testimony.

LEARNING FROM THE FIRST CHRISTIANS

Study the following passages related to the early church in the book Acts. Note in each passage how the church prayed, dealt with conflict, shared the gospel, and loved each other. Then write down any insights that could help guide the life and ministry of the church you attend.

Passage	Insight	How this could impact the church today
Acts 2:42–47		
Acts 4:23–37		
Acts 6:1–7		
Acts 12:1–19		
Acts 13:1–3		

Send your insights to your small group members and let them learn what you learned through your study in the book of Acts.

If we lose the element of prayer, how can we call ourselves a "New Testament church"?

BREAKING DOWN BARRIERS

There are many barriers to prayer in our lives and churches. Take time to reflect on the five barriers listed below and on the following pages and identify ways they might exist in your life. Then come up with at least two ways you could break down each of these barriers.

BARRIER #1: Slander

- How it shows up in your life:

- Two ways you could break down this barrier:

BARRIER #2: Gossip

- How it shows up in your life:

- Two ways you could break down this barrier:

BARRIER #3: Unforgiveness

➤ How it shows up in your life:

➤ Two ways you could break down this barrier:

BARRIER #4: Negative Talk

➤ How it shows up in your life:

➤ Two ways you could break down this barrier:

BARRIER #5: Complaining

➤ How it shows up in your life:

➤ Two ways you could break down this barrier:

Instead of texting the universe, why don't we talk more to God?

LIFTING UP UNIFIERS

Although there are behaviors that can become a barrier to the work of the Holy Spirit, there are also behaviors that can propel you forward in prayer and invite the fullness of the Spirit to fill your life, home, and church. Identify where each of the following five "unifiers" exist in your life, and then set goals for how you can develop and expand them.

UNIFIER #1: Love

➤ How this exists in your life:

- How you can develop and grow this behavior:

UNIFIER #2: Humility

- How this exists in your life:

- How you can develop and grow this behavior:

UNIFIER #3: Forgiveness

- How this exists in your life:

- How you can develop and grow this behavior:

UNIFIER #4: Mutual Respect

- How this exists in your life:

- How you can develop and grow this behavior:

UNIFIER #5: Mercy

- How this exists in your life:

- How you can develop and grow this behavior:

The Holy Spirit is God's only agent on earth. Any good that is going to happen has to be done by the Holy Spirit.

JOURNAL, REFLECTIONS, AND NOTES

As you reflect on what God is teaching you through this session, use the space below to write any key points or questions you want to mention to your group leader or fellow group members in the coming days.

Additional Resources for Group Leaders

Thank you for your willingness to lead a group through *Life-Changing Prayer*! What you have chosen to do is important, and much good fruit can come from studies like this. The rewards of being a leader are different from those of participating, and we hope that as you lead you will find your own walk with Jesus deepened by this experience.

Life-Changing Prayer is a six-session study built around video content and small-group interaction. As the group leader, imagine yourself as the host of a dinner party. Your job is to take care of your guests by managing all the behind-the-scenes details so that as your guests arrive, they can focus on one another and on interaction around the topic.

As the group leader, your role is *not* to answer all the questions or reteach the content—the video and study guide will do most of that work. Your job is to guide the experience and cultivate your small group into a kind of teaching community. This will make it a place for members to process, question, and reflect—not receive more instruction.

There are several elements in this leader's guide that will help you as you structure your study and reflection time, so follow along and take advantage of each one.

BEFORE YOU BEGIN

Before your first meeting, make sure the group members have a copy of this study guide so they can follow along and have their answers written out ahead of time. Alternately, you can hand out the study guides at your first meeting and give the group members some time to look over the material and ask any preliminary questions. During your first meeting, be sure to send a sheet around the room and have the members write down their name, phone number, and email address so you can keep in touch with them during the week.

Generally, the ideal size for a group is between eight to ten people, which ensures everyone will have enough time to participate in discussions. If you have more people, you might want to break up the main group into smaller subgroups. Encourage those who show up at the first meeting to commit to attending the duration of the study, as this will help the group members get to know each other, create stability for the group, and help you know how to prepare each week.

Each of the sessions begins with an opening reflection. The questions that follow in the "Talk About It" section serve as an icebreaker to get the group members thinking about the topic. Some people may want to tell a long story in response to one of these questions, but the goal is to keep the answers brief. Ideally, you want everyone in the group to get a chance to answer, so try to keep the responses to a minute or less. If you have talkative group members, say up front that everyone needs to limit their answer to one minute.

Give the group members a chance to answer, but tell them to feel free to pass if they wish. With the rest of the study, it's generally not a good idea to have everyone answer every question—a free-flowing discussion is more desirable. But with the opening icebreaker questions, you can go around the circle. Encourage shy people to share, but don't force them.

Before your first meeting, let the group members know that each session contains several between-sessions activities that they can complete during the week. While these are optional exercises, they will help the members cement the concepts presented during the group study time and encourage them to spend time each day in God's Word. Also invite members to bring any questions and insights they uncovered while reading to your next meeting, especially if they had a breakthrough moment or didn't understand something.

WEEKLY PREPARATION

As the leader, there are a few things you should do to prepare for each meeting:

- *Read through the session.* This will help you to become familiar with the content and know how to structure the discussion times.
- *Decide which questions you definitely want to discuss.* Based on the amount and length of group discussion, you may not be able to get through all of the Bible study and group discussion questions, so choose four to five questions that you definitely want to cover.
- *Be familiar with the questions you want to discuss.* When the group meets you'll be watching the clock, so you want to make sure you are familiar with the questions you have selected. In this way, you'll ensure you have the material more deeply in your mind than your group members.
- *Pray for your group.* Pray for your group members throughout the week and ask God to lead them as they study his Word.
- *Bring extra supplies to your meeting.* The members should bring their own pens for writing notes, but it's a good idea to have extras available for those who forget. You may also want to bring paper and additional Bibles.

STRUCTURING THE DISCUSSION TIME

You will need to determine with your group how long you want to meet each week so you can plan your time accordingly. Generally, most groups like to meet for either sixty minutes or ninety minutes, so you could use one of the following schedules:

As the group leader, it is up to you to keep track of the time and keep things moving along according to your schedule. You might want to set a timer for each segment so both you and the group members know when your time is up. (Note there are some good phone apps for timers that play a gentle chime or other pleasant sound instead of a disruptive noise.)

Section	**60 Minutes**	**90 Minutes**
WELCOME (members arrive and get settled)	5 minutes	10 minutes
ICEBREAKER (discuss one or both of opening questions for the session)	10 minutes	15 minutes
VIDEO (watch the teaching segment together and take notes)	15 minutes	15 minutes
DISCUSSION (discuss the Bible study questions you selected ahead of time)	25 minutes	40 minutes
PRAYER/CLOSING (pray together as a group and dismiss)	5 minutes	10 minutes

Don't be concerned if the group members are quiet or slow to share. People are often quiet when they are pulling together their ideas, and this might be a new experience for them. Just ask a question and let it hang in the air until someone shares. You can then say, "Thank you. What about others? What came to you when you watched that portion of the video?"

Note that in many cases there will be no one "right" answer to the question the group will be discussing. Answers will vary, especially when the group members are being asked to share their personal experiences.

GROUP DYNAMICS

Leading a group through *Life-Changing Prayer* will prove to be highly rewarding both to you and your group members. However, this doesn't mean you will not encounter any challenges along the way! Discussions can get off track. Group members may not be sensitive to the needs and ideas of others. Some might worry they will be expected to talk about matters that make them feel awkward. Others may express comments that result in disagreements. To help ease this strain on you and the group, consider the following ground rules:

- When someone raises a question or comment that is off the main topic, suggest you deal with it another time, or if you feel led to go in that direction, let the group know you will be spending some time discussing it.
- If someone asks a question you don't know how to answer, admit it and move on. If applicable, research the answer before the next meeting and follow up with the questioner.
- At your discretion, feel free to invite group members to comment on questions that call for personal experience.
- If you find one or two people are dominating the discussion time, direct a few questions to others in the group. Outside the main group time, ask the more dominating members to help you draw out the quieter ones. Work to make them a part of the solution instead of the problem.

- When a disagreement occurs, encourage the group members to process the matter in love. Encourage those on opposite sides to restate what they heard the other side say about the matter, and then invite each side to evaluate if that perception is accurate. Lead the group in examining other Scriptures related to the topic and look for common ground.

When any of these issues arise, encourage your group members to follow these words from the Bible: "Love one another" (John 13:34); "If it is possible, as far as it depends on you, live at peace with everyone" (Romans 12:18); and "Be quick to listen, slow to speak and slow to become angry" (James 1:19). This will make your group time more rewarding and beneficial for everyone who attends.

Thank you again for your willingness to lead your group. May God reward your efforts and dedication and make your time together in *Life-Changing Prayer* fruitful for his kingdom.

When God's Spirit Moves Video Study

Six Sessions on the Life-Changing Power of the Holy Spirit

Jim Cymbala with Dean Merrill

In this six-session small group Bible study (video sold separately), pastor and bestselling author Jim Cymbala explores the person and work of the Holy Spirit to bring a fresh sense of God's power to your church and your life.

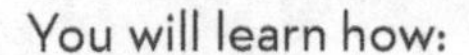

You will learn how:

- To make room for the Spirit's action in your life and in your church
- God wants to work through your gifts and talents to enable you to do what only he can do
- To listen for the voice of the Spirit in prayer and how to apply God's Word to your life
- The Spirit can bring healing to your body, your emotions, and your relationships; how a life lived in the presence of the Spirit can transform the church and the world

Your church can become a place where people regularly experience God's presence and his power.

Sessions include:

1. Agent in the Shadows
2. Power Source
3. The Best Bible Teacher
4. Water, Wind, and Fire
5. Who's in Control?
6. Help When We Need It Most

Appendix: A Long Night in Indianapolis

Available in stores and online!